*Roller-Skating Notes*

# *Roller-Skating Notes*

*poems by*

Nina Zivancevic

Coolgrove Press

Copyright © 2021 Nina Zivancevic

Coolgrove Press, an imprint of
Cool Grove Publishing, Inc. New York.
512 Argyle Road, Brooklyn, NY 11218
All rights reserved under the International and
 Pan-American Copyright Conventions.
www.coolgrove.com
For permissions and other inquiries write to info@coolgrove.com

   ISBN 13: 978-1-887276-40-5
   Library of Congress Control Number: 2021937450

   This book is distributed to the trade by Ingram Spark


Cover art by
Antonia Alexandra Klimenko

   Coolgrove happy to announce,
   Nina Zivancevic is the winner of the
   2021 CENTRE NATIONAL DU LIVRE [CNL]
   grant for creative writing (poetry domain).

   She feels specialy honored to receive it for her project,
   titled <u>The Source of Light</u> in which she describes
   poetry as the only source of light in these times when
   so many people on our planet live in disgrace and total
   darkness. She was inspired by the SYRIAN poet
   Nouri al-Jarrah who exclaimed: poetry is the only
   source of Light!


Media alchemy by Kiku

Coolgrove Press

This book is dedicated to the magazines, their readers and editors who had honored my voice in poetry before it hit the page in the following magazines: *The Wolf, The Opiate, Maintenant, Les Intempestives, Minor Literature(s), Cold Lips, Alienist, Polja, Sent, Enklava 2, Theodorazine, La Rose de Personne, LoveLove, Libartes, Otoliths* and *Paris Lit Up*.

Nina Zivancevic

Other books by Nina Zivancevic

*Death of New York City* (poetry)

*More or Less Urgent* (poetry)

*I Was This War Reporter in Egypt* (poetry)

*Letters to Myself* (poetry)

*Sous le Signe de Cyber-Cybèle* (poetry)

*L'amour n'est qu'un mot* (poetry)

*Sonnets en avion* (poetry)

*Inside & Out of Byzantium* (short stories)

*Living on Air* (novel)

*Crnjanski: La Serbie, l'Exile et le Retour* (monography)

*11 Femmes Artistes Slaves et Nomades* (essays)

*Roller-Skating Notes*

*Table of Contents*

ROLLER-SKATING NOTES . . . . . . . . . . . . . . . . . . . . . . . . . . . . . . . . *1*
MADE UP MY MIND . . . . . . . . . . . . . . . . . . . . . . . . . . . . . . . . *3*
INSTEAD OF A PHOTO OR A DRAWING, ON CHRISTMAS EVENING . . . . . . . . . . . . . . . . . . . . . . . . . . . . . . . . *6*
ELYSIAN FIELDS OF POWER . . . . . . . . . . . . . . . . . . . . . . . . . . . . . . . . *8*
ALBA AVIS . . . . . . . . . . . . . . . . . . . . . . . . . . . . . . . . . . . . . . . . . . . . . *10*
A LIMINE . . . . . . . . . . . . . . . . . . . . . . . . . . . . . . . . . . . . . . . . . . . . . . *12*
SAMSARA . . . . . . . . . . . . . . . . . . . . . . . . . . . . . . . . . . . . . . . . . . . . *14*
WAR DRUMS OR *LE CONTRE-ATAQUE D'EMPIRE* . . . . . . . . . . *15*
THE RAVEN . . . . . . . . . . . . . . . . . . . . . . . . . . . . . . . . . . . . . . . . . . *19*
A SO CALLED LOVE-POEM . . . . . . . . . . . . . . . . . . . . . . . . . . . . . *20*
ACTIVE ACTIVIST PERFORMING ACTION . . . . . . . . . . . . . . . . . *21*
CEDRIC HERROU IS MY HERO . . . . . . . . . . . . . . . . . . . . . . . . . *23*
DROP OF SPANISH BLOOD . . . . . . . . . . . . . . . . . . . . . . . . . . . . *24*
IMMACULATE OSMOSIS . . . . . . . . . . . . . . . . . . . . . . . . . . . . . . *26*
THE ISLAND (*KORKYRA NEGRA*) . . . . . . . . . . . . . . . . . . . . . . . . *27*
POSTED FOR ETERNIT . . . . . . . . . . . . . . . . . . . . . . . . . . . . . . . . *33*
SYRIAN DARK, VERY DARK BUT STILL A SONG . . . . . . . . . . . *35*
THE UNCOMPROMISED ONE . . . . . . . . . . . . . . . . . . . . . . . . . . *37*
WE ARE PUSHING THIS N-TIETH EXILE . . . . . . . . . . . . . . . . . . *39*
CONFESSIONS OF A FALLEN ANGEL
      NIETZSCHEAN SONG . . . . . . . . . . . . . . . . . . . . . . . . . . *45*
CHOPIN . . . . . . . . . . . . . . . . . . . . . . . . . . . . . . . . . . . . . . . . . . . . *47*
HANNAH ARENDT . . . . . . . . . . . . . . . . . . . . . . . . . . . . . . . . . . . *49*
SMARTPHONE . . . . . . . . . . . . . . . . . . . . . . . . . . . . . . . . . . . . . . *51*
IF I WERE TO PAINT . . . . . . . . . . . . . . . . . . . . . . . . . . . . . . . . . . *52*
RELIGIOUS DREAM . . . . . . . . . . . . . . . . . . . . . . . . . . . . . . . . . . *53*
POLITICALLY CORRECT . . . . . . . . . . . . . . . . . . . . . . . . . . . . . . . *55*

## Nina Zivancevic

| | |
|---|---|
| FRANC LISZT'S HOUSE. | 56 |
| MAYBE THE SPRING | 57 |
| THERE'S SOMETHING | 59 |
| BERGSON, ON THE EDGE OF POSITIVE THINKING | 60 |
| IF. | 61 |
| SOON I'LL BE BACK | 62 |
| AN OPEN LETTER TO A VERY VERY STRAWBERRY FRIEND. | 63 |
| CONTACT IMPROVISATION | 64 |
| FOR MY DEAD LOST AND FORLORN FRIEN | 65 |
| ERRARE HUMANUM EST, PERSEVERARE DIABOLICUM | 67 |
| IT'S A HOLLYWOOD DRAMA. | 69 |
| MY CHILDHOOD | 71 |
| PAPA ERIC LE TENDRE AND JOAQUÍN GUZMAN (EL CHAPO) ARE MY HEROS | 2 |
| EL CHAPO | 73 |
| THE BALLAD OF STENKA RAZIN. | 5 |
| THEM RUSSIANS. | 77 |
| TRIPLE SORROW. | 79 |
| NOW YOU SEE IT—NOW YOU DON'T SEE I | 81 |
| POEM FOR EM | 83 |
| ABJECT/DÉBRIS ART 1 | 89 |
| ABJECT/DEBRIS 2. | 87 |
| PRAGUE 89 .BUDAPEST BUKAREST WARSOVIE BELGRADE. | 91 |
| PARIS IS BURNING. | 93 |
| ABOUT THE AUTHOR | 96 |

*Roller-Skating Notes*

## ROLLER-SKATING NOTES

It is so much better to get a pair of roller-skates
   and set a poem free,

it is so much more interesting to see some friends once a year,
it is so much mucho painful to see some people every day
it is certainly much more subliminal to be left alone
write diaries or read an airconditioned Blaise Cendrars,
it is certainly much more useful to lie down, not
move, touch the earth, kiss the floor, embrace the door and
   much  more

perhaps just howl or hold someone dear to you,
it is certainly much more practical to fumble through invoices,
legal documents or unfinished galleys of a commercial
   publisher,

it is certainly much more satisfying to sit on a Kandahar
   balcony,

patting an Afghani hound in a lazy crystalline afternoon dusk,
it is certainly much more romantic to be Dracula's lover or
Voltaire's fellow-talker in a European gloomy castle,
or drink beer at CBGB's with your ball chain and leather
   psychedelic pals,

evidently, it takes much more effort to sign petitions

## Nina Zivancevic

   to set prisoners free, write phony mail

to iron-curtain cordial officials or answer useless or urgent
calls when your heart is on fire,
and it's even more prestigious to keep up with the
   Tennessee

Song Lyrics contests or with scoops of the news from
   various

organizational gatherings claiming that you can still
print whatever you think
about the guy who stopped me on a street this morning
yelling out prophetic words at me and the one
I remembered was meant to hit me hard
below every inch of the belt
IF YOU wanna skate, he said,
YOU HAVE TO HAVE AN ATTITUDE
and this glorious city, smaller than life,
will not let your poem
fly away with that one

*Roller-Skating Notes*

## I MADE UP MY MIND
## I'M LEAVING NEW YORK

Because I'm tired of looking at sky in rectangular concrete chips,

Because F. Scott Fitzgerald & Mr. West were starving for two years while

Diving in a swimming pool

Because I'm not Greta Garbo and I don't want to be alone

In my Brooklyn chicken- poxed incense impregnated $7.000000 a month apartment

Because the Marx brothers are not doing Animal Crackers this year on

Broadway, no rip ridin' Will Rogers sermonizing for Flo Ziegfeld

Because the porcelain blue sky is hard to find aside from the air in between

Why poor slum downtown reflects the cruel sins of my admirers

When it's dawning in the blissful blessing of my aspirins

Nina Zivancevic

New Year's Day
Ding dong ding dong!
In twenty months of break dancing
In twenty moths three periods missing due to tingling
   poisonous metal effect

Of Avenue Mayor Koch gentrification
I am not Atlas in Rockefeller Center! But I am not Lana
   Turner either;

Thirty first is dead! Out with a zero and into the orbit-
There is a day tender as saffron: TODAY
Now that all of the pages are gone from my detective
   murder mystery

Calendar pastiche, the thing just says the word "today"
White letters on black cardboard, with a capital T., NYC
I am tremendously worried by my constant lack of Him
it was a temporary relief, a little night work because I
can't sleep

Because there are too many things that bother me like
why do we
Have to live like rats? No Fred & Adele in taps over on
   42$^{nd}$ & Sunset Blvd.

Gloria Swanson got $900000 from Paramount in 1934
While I earn- "I don' even want to mention that" and
Lana Turner had too many genuine fits for poodles and
Liz Taylor had 900 fur coats but did not overdose like

## Roller-Skating Notes

Judy
   Garland of the flowers!
And God bless Betty Ford, Happy Rockefeller, DeWolf
   Hopper
Abbe who says "Everybody's gonna die for Nicaragua, but
   they
Won't bury even their next door neighbor",
What a bunch of horseshit lined 2$^{nd}$ Avenue in 1934 when
Gentlemen took the curbside for ladies and
Gentlemen please welcome
   This new year,
It's a pleasure to be here I've made up my mind I'm
   definitively leaving
(I stole that from Groucho I guess)

*On New Year's eve in Holy-wood, 3 hours before*
*Steve de Souza's party.*

Nina Zivancevic

## INSTEAD OF A PHOTO OR A DRAWING, ON CHRISTMAS EVENING
*(for Yasha, Olivera eventually)*

Don't get me wrong-
The "wrong" sometimes gets hold of us,
Rears its ugly head
And then disaster, stupidity…

The light of reason is flooding my room now,
Then the ante-chamber and the entire church
Of my goodwill where the secret altar burns,
The innermost chapel of my heart,
You are in it too, shiny with that light
Brighter than the flames,
Dangerous to reach and lost to my touch

You dwelled in it for quite a while,
Not paying the rent, ignoring the angels
Their tired messages, the price was too high
The ossified bone shell, expensive ivory-tower
In which our hearts used to speak, in rumours

## Roller-Skating Notes

Or in whispers, crying out loud, cackling,
Those hearts burned to ashes and then the smoke
Raising above the candles, floating in the air,
Yes, constantly floating, but what else
Could they do?

Nina Zivancevic

## ELYSIAN FIELDS OF POWER
*(For Stephanette, Ivana eventually)*

So, Tiny Tom and Speedy Gonzales
Have had a Lab,
It was pretty much a physical thing,
They tried to outdo the topology of a body in space
From person A to person B ran the 'power-field of
a person', so how would we envelope them
into our power-circle, if we were to say
'I'm taking over a situation'?
then
You would say 'I don't want to take a person
In my power-field, I want them to be free,
And besides, I'm not Pina Bausch or Vito Acconci',

Documentation is more a referent than a remainder
And performance means
There's an audience,
An event is an accident sometimes
And sometimes it's steady and sleepy, like a video;
There may be people or not

## Roller-Skating Notes

A couple of technical by-products
But what always really counts is people
Who make decision whether
to be there or not to be
as we're making a private
out of their public space
and
not everyone can get it...
we are just trying to become these buildings
themselves, a part of the architectural landscape,
surroundings   which is
the Other

## ALBA AVIS

(for Claude*)

*Aliéna ne cures!*
*Aliéna negotia non curare…*

And you take care of the aliens,
Of their alien wishes and affairs,
What thunder has struck your
Hollow brow?
Your thought
Dwelling between a void and
Latin quotations, my clear alien
Friend whom I befriended in
The most alien hour of my
Late springtime …
There is a fountain in Rome
Where the young brides used to drink water
So that they could have sons only;

If you're not my belated father, then
You are probably my new-born son,
Caught in the web of summer insects

## Roller-Skating Notes

Craving for the morning light...

When the dinner's over
And the stories got burnt to ashes,
We leave messages to one another:
That the wax had melted down,
That the bulls got pierced by sunshine
That the wine's red and the crystal transparent
We say so many things
          But the silence remains
While at the same time encouraging us to ride on
As we had already mounted
          That melancholy horse again...

*"Claudius, the one who's always closed"*

Nina Zivancevic

## A LIMINE
(should I refuse from the start)
*For Eric-(Aesotheric) Lerner*

Perhaps I should say 'no' from the start
To this lonely year full of scaffolds
When energy flows in and out,
Like cold water oozing through a faucet;
Icy rain and snowfields, mangos for
Breakfast for our sparkling imagination,
—this is my second poem for you, my
Long-standing pal of abused poetry,
I see you attend a workshop of good manners
And bad intentions, you would not shave
And hated washing your hair, and I was
Always there, absent-minded,
Trying to bring several friends back to life,
Those who appeared, but then disappeared in
The daily theatre of our vowels
And rusty consonants full of smoke.
One of them had a stroke,
And another one a jaw cancer, and the third one,
Oh, that one never died.
He ate daisies and cucumbers for lunch, and

## *Roller-Skating Notes*

I spoke to him in person, while I was dwelling
High, above in the sky.
You say you miss him a lot, I say: it's fabulous
That we've ever met, appeared and then disappeared
On the sunny side of the street; it's snowing a lot
Around here  and all the smudges
Around my eyes remain prominent and natural by now…
There is no other Christmas gift for you
But this song and you know its special tune
So
   you
      can
         sing
            it

Nina Zivancevic

## SAMSARA
(from Dechen Padmo)

Samsara is killing us-
Too much talk about money and its
neoliberal
Issues, too much talk and
Worry, too much fear,
The essential slips away
The existential crawls in
We will survive
And then- what else- die
Under the kind
and watchful
Eye of our good
Lord Tcherenzi

*Roller-Skating Notes*

### WAR DRUMS or
### LE CONTRE-ATAQUE D'EMPIRE
(for my son)

DOOM DOOM DOOM ACHOOUM !
DUMB   DUMB   DUMB   DUMB !
The drums of war are having fun …

It is so dumb to suffer this doom
For so many times throughout history
Tucidides hated it, the Romans grasped for it
It's only they had more style in faking the greatness
Of their dumb empire when they conquered Carthage
Recently known as Lebanon with its blisters and horror and worries…

DOOM DOOM DOOM ACHOOUM !
DUMB   DUMB   DUMB   DUMB !
There is a fear there in hurting others
Fear of starvation and an infantile kick-
"I'm gonna conquer everyone, I'm gonna be better"
And false modesty is just a mode to say that you are really better
And more powerful than the enemy

But the perverse thing—when one comes to think of this
century
Is  selling the arms to the Carthaginians then persuading
them to attack the others
Just out of fear and spite and false feeling of might
An old trick a dope dealer would teach you in the street,
age ten
Can never sell things and buy wisdom at the same time,
At the same time the drums of war ( or is it just a bad
economy deal and panic?)

The drums beat DUMB DUMB DUMB DUMB
SCUM   SCUM        SCUM        SCUM
DOOM DOOM DOOM DOOM
Bloody soldiers and corpses enter everyone's room
I was so crushed when NATO bombed my home town
I could barely got my own mother out of that place
And I believed ! Fool that I was, that
I would never speak a word of English again
My shrink had told me: distance yourself from
Yourself and don't be so DUMB    DUMB     DUMB
DUMB

Like the rest of this scum !
Doomed to walk in this ancient town and see that
Those who clone new human beings will  soon destroy
them

### Roller-Skating Notes

And those who pay taxes will buy the axes and will
Destroy the road to Carthage—Flaubert wrote Sallambo
And the Ridiculous Theatre staged it, than the actor died
And a president had a try, the Greeks tried to teach the
   Romans how

To think—whatever they learnt from the Persians,
The Persians settled along the West Coast in the U.S. and
   started paying

Their taxes, oh how they were
DUMB     DUMB     DUMB    shook by their Doom
   looking for a crumb !

Byzantium crushed to ashes, the Ottoman heroes
   fearing the Kurds !


DUMB DUMB DUMB DUMB—forget about the
DOOM DOOM DOOM DOO—the formula is easy :
Go and learn your history lesson—a happy transit will
Calm your passion, dry your tears and drown your fears,
A reminder for the small ones : on the top of the theater
   board

An ancient alphabet spells the letters : THE EMPIRE
STRIKES BACK !

(the director is Greek – has something to teach us: go home
   and

## Nina Zivancevic

turn your TV on : instead of the stars up there over that ancient Iraqi land

you might spot the bombs made of depleted
(impoverished Uranium)
and nobody knows how they got there nor what to do with them after all

DOOM DOOM DOOM DOOM
DUMB DUMB DUMB DUMB the drums of war
Are having fun.

## THE RAVEN
### (after E.A. Poe)

*And it does not mean that*
*all the things won't return with their dreadful refrain 'never*
*more', remember René Char who said that "everything that was*
*taken was returned to him, even his little red truck,"*
*but what it means is they won't come back with that crazy,*
*insane but to me so dear, adorable in-ten-si-ty;*

*Oh, your pupil, raven, glistening in your oily eye–*
*shows you at your best, the perfect, arrogant and abusive creature,*
*domineering; your shape of a lonely bird–foreboding,*
*your eye, translucent and penetrating, observes me intensely*
*just this morning, as you land on my Kerala terrace,*
*yes you do and then take fruits from my palm, I've just cut it*
*for you,  as you gobble these pieces from my hand,*
*I hear myself whispering semi-absently*
*"never more," "never more"…*

Nina Zivancevic

## A SO CALLED LOVE-POEM

*for MJL*

Anyways
Ill always keep a stunt in yr circus
Thanks for keeping that trapeze net for me
That's why i love you
as only you allow me to perform
without that net.
And when i'm just about to break my neck
You place the palm of your hand
above the ground

## Roller-Skating Notes

### ACTIVE ACTIVIST PERFORMING ACTION

You can put these inverted commas wherever you like,
above any act or action of mine,
The entire cities of Paris, London or Belgrade are my daily stage
where i pound the streets and fill out the refugees' cups with money
As i try not to insult them i tell them
First : *seelaam aleicum*
And when some respond with *aleicum selaam*
Some also add *Shukran*
And to some of them i say
*Afuan* and some of them ask
in English where do i come from
And to some of them i answer
I was born in the state of disgust
And to some of them i say
I was born in a dessert
And to some of them
I say i was born in the midst of
Neoliberal madness
And some of them do think

# Nina Zivancevic

That i am crazy
And some of them think that
I fell in the state of total disgrace
And some of them pat my hand as if
It were Fatima's in disguise of an angel
And so i know
That i have no other choice
But to return home B like broke
T like tired
M like moved to tears
No, i m not an anarchist
My grandfather did it for me
Come to think of it
Now that i'm at home
All alone..

*Roller-Skating Notes*

## CEDRIC HERROU IS MY HERO

Cedric Herrou
Is my hero
 he led 123 migrants
To find shelter and food near Marseille and then he was arrested
8 months of prison
As it is against the 2012 law to help
Migrants in distress
Or should i spell it out in
Different languages:
Evil spreads like a poisonous web
All over this place

Nina Zivancevic

## DROP OF SPANISH BLOOD
(a migrant's story)

I see your rage

You poor migrant's son

Your resplendent beauty as you

Defend my honor

In front of that large bureaucratic stupidity

I knew you would have to revenge on those

Who have been humiliating me since the day one:

You were about to leave my stomach and I couldn't ask

For water

The nurses ignored me, I was hysteric

On the verge of tears

I was changing your diapers on a bus to Hungary

When they wanted to throw us out

From the bus

And then much later

The police officers were asking me if I spoke

To you in French, for the sake of better integration;

No one has ever seen my tears but you

At night when I was reading and rereading the French dictionary

I thought I was going insane

## *Roller-Skating Notes*

And today flashing all these beautiful
Polite and polished idioms in your father-tongue
You have fought for my rights, resilient poet
that you are, disheveled , brilliant and modest
you've noticed : less is always more,
it survives in winter
in my private language of oblivion
it's just a language, and the meaning remains hidden
to those who have never moved
out of their walled up chambers
and their
tucked up destiny

## Nina Zivancevic

## IMMACULATE OSMOSIS

Whenever I look at you

You look at me

Whenever you start to cough

I sneeze

You eat from my plate

I eat from yours

I sit on your lap

You sit on my shoe

My eyes are deep

And yours are light blue

You talk history of ideas

I talk the ideas in history

I like a big black cock

You like it too

You carry my weight after midnight

I carry your weight before dawn

You give me shit

I give you shit

And this immense love of freedom,

I'm giving to you, Hypocrite!!

*Roller-Skating Notes*

## THE ISLAND
### (KORKYRA NEGRA)

*(For Rajka Gorup, my sister "in arms" and in exile)*

I.

Conveyed by Virgin Mary and the angels of Dubrovnik—
I talk to

People in their mother tongue-Serbian accent though, no one is willing

To sell me a bus-ticket or any food, no porter, no luggage space, I talk in twisted tongues

With the buried enemies, buried hopes, for the improvement, split minds, divided

Feelings, twisted intentions, sick memories, "divide et impera", "idis redibis…"

*Nunquam nunquam nunquam*
Never did I want to come to this island built
Of white foam frothy *nunquams*
I divided
I Split I Dubrovnik I banana
I entered the crystals
Built of foam and glass I saw the shadow of the medieval courtyard

## Nina Zivancevic

Huge poplars closed over our heads like the ones in
  Tuscany

Hit by an instant heat… like the one in Tel Amarna
Before the Moslem Brothers came to power and before
  the Christians

Lost their religious marbles and beads,
one more time…


II. He came from that island,
A poet/ painter who has deceived me
Who was deceived by the notion of friendship
And what it meant.
It rose to the sky resembling a wave-crest
Between now and then, between Dubrovnik and
  Korchula,

Orebic it was called then.
I will always be going to visit
His log-cabin and the seagulls nesting there…
He held my hand against the mast
Leaned against the boat's rudder, age 4,
He gave me a yellow flower which
I have been carrying in my heart.
He came from that island, that crass,
A poet painter who had deceived me
Who was also deceived by the notion
Of friendship, starry faces, to the sky which looks like

*Roller-Skating Notes*

The wave's crest, between now and then, between Dubrovnik

And Korchula, Orebic, it was called then…


III.

Fatamorgana's Daughter
The parakeets would conquer the air,
The cats would rule the earth, the snakes
Would dig the ground, my voice would muster
The Howl and shriek , the fogs would cover the earth
Fuzzy clouds wrapping your memory
The just would rake the soil
And you would plant the seeds of knowledge
Thin and shiny, like the Inka's golden pectoral,
The accounts had already been settled
Between me and you
Better than those of the Quipus Indians
Come to my garden, the lavenders are in bloom,
You said, I will never deceive you, the crickets
Went on chirping, their silly song
Making our neighbors luminous and happy,
The magnolias descending in white petals..
Come to my garden, you said, before
You died in my arms,
the sick rotting smell of the wisterias

as if you should never deceive the momentum
like the sun glistening over the peninsula Peljesac,
steady and shiny, and the crickets went on
and on, with their silly song,
the Bougainvillea in all shades of purple
like a cut-out taken out of Enki Bilal's movie…


IV.
Sometimes I see
this landscape in my dreams…
mother is young and pretty
and always away in a special
outdoor garden with my dad,
they have
just made love and
I run towards them: Mom, Dad,
I am going to marry my cousin Andrea!
The elder auntie enters with a platter
Of grapes and olives
And the younger one takes my hand:
She would take me to see captain Marco
Polo's house nested sheer turquoise,
Its sturdy walls and the pirate's bay
Long before China became an export-import market
Advertising the silicone and the plastics..
No one can come and sit in our summer house
Before 6pm or 7,

## Roller-Skating Notes

The palms the olive trees and the almonds
Repeat themselves in steady lines
Steady order conservative winds religions
Of the diverse climate


V.

The Danger
But the danger lies hidden in there
He is of the age when they crucified Christ
And me dancing like Salomé the dance of 1000 veils
This one has fell off let's face the truth
I cannot open my mouth without sounding like a
Murderer of children's dreams here
In this region my accents stinks and is foul like a corpse
In summer so what do we do
My friend B. and I, ? We speak English and Swedish and Urdu
So that the birds would understand us
So that the local population would not spit at us
Saying like: OOOOHH—these two are two
Full-blooded SERBS!! Now they will eat our cats and devour our dogs,
they will slash our throats and drink our blood for
   breakfast with toasted

Buns or without these buns with butter…
Civil war is a son of a bitch

civil war is a son of a bitch
civil war is a son of.
And I will leave to someone else someone like
Bob Wilson, to stage the Civil Wars,
As I try, I try and try
I try... to forget all about them!!
And the delicate poetess from the island has uttered:
Oh, let me read my poems about Srebrenica to you,
And let me read my poems about the civil wars to you,
And I replied :
OK, just do it, why not--
It took her all her strength to force herself
To read them out to me,
As it took all my force and strength
To hear all her poems she was about to read
It took us so long to write these poems
About Srebrenica,
Jasenovac and Auschwitz
After Srebrenica , Jasenovac and Auschwitz had happened
And it took us so much strength and courage to listen to the poetry

about Srebrenica,
Jasenovac and Auschwitz
It took us so much courage to live poetry
after Srebrenica ... Jasenovac and...

*Roller-Skating Notes*

## POSTED FOR ETERNITY

Stay well

Be happy

Don't be sacrificial

Eat no ideology

Breath fresh sentence

Let yourself go

Change your underwear

Empty your mind

From time to time- turn around

Love this world.

Don't be pompous.

Now, turn around again,

Forget about the form

Tend to the content,

Be yourself content in it

Love your parents

Don't hate the different nor *la difference*

Get yourself some kids.

Dance yourself to death,

Always swim upward against the tide.

Forget about art

## Nina Zivancevic

Try to love habit
Wear soft shoes
Stay warm- hearted
Forget about regrets,
You're lucky,

You'll never die!

*Roller-Skating Notes*

## SYRIAN DARK, VERY DARK BUT STILL A SONG…

According to data gathered by UNHCR, so far this year more than 200,000 Syrians have arrived in Europe, adding to the 230,000 already there.

<u>This new influx amounts to roughly 5 per cent of the total number of Syrian refugees, but that 5 per cent has captured most of the media coverage: life jackets strewn across the beaches of Lesbos and Kos;</u>

the body of the drowned toddler, Alan Kurdi, washed up on a Turkish beach; impromptu tent cities in public parks in Athens; police batons in Macedonia, tear gas and razor-wire fences in Hungary; and an epic march towards Western Europe.

There is a Syrian refugee crisis and a European border crisis and the one cannot be reduced to the other.

The vast majority of the four million refugees are living in countries on Syria's borders. <u>Turkey is home to an estimated two million,</u>

<u>Jordan 1.4 million and Lebanon 1.2 million.
Russia, Iran, the US, Britain and the Gulf States have all intervened in the conflict,</u> but none has been willing to accept large numbers of Syrian refugees on their own territory.

To date, the US has resettled around 1500 Syrians, while Britain has only recently committed to resettling 20,000 over the next five years.


The Gulf States have resettled none, although Saudi Arabia claims to have allowed in anywhere between 500,000 and 2.5 million Syrians as 'migrant workers'. The number depends on which government official you listen to.

*Roller-Skating Notes*

## THE UNCOMPROMISED ONE

The highest peak of osmosis
With the lady who some people  called mr james
His sense of unity his baroque sentiment of justice
   versus passion
that 's always between us- though we've never met
neither in the real
nor symbolic
oh imaginary worlds
around us , so
we've been meeting in
the back alleys of pure thought
where daisies sleep
and our profound desire
for metaphysics
so what is a girl
without her home country?
What's a child without a desire?
what is a man without
metaphysics?
can  you answer  this:
oh

# Nina Zivancevic

but you,
 have every question
for every answer
at least this time
try to enter
this daisyland full of horror
your meta-world
sprinkled with smileys
and some pink pink
pink kink
where you sink
and hang on
that Broadway mink
 stretched on that
chewing-gum

## Roller-Skating Notes

### WE ARE PUSHING THIS N-TIETH EXILE
*For my anarcho-anthropologist camarade in exile,*
*brother in arms, David Graeber*

We are all 99 percent
And I am 100 percent sure
That exile is a chained melody, babble in chains
Transformational grammar in pain
Weak thought in labor
Laughter in distress
Smile in despair
Love was in the air but high anxiety
Got hold of it,
The better part of my *Id* wanted
To quit this place of forlorn hopes
moons ago,
Much earlier than your Trintignant unique image got to these shores
Oh, when you see, my king D.,
my high-school Levinasian royalty,
A Mabuhay forest moving to your private garden you should run away,
A field-work for eternity, seashells instead of money
Getting paid in spices and sunglasses

## Nina Zivancevic

Cleaning the filthiest gutters in this new land
Draining your students minds for posterity
Please don't cry when nobody sees you-
The spiritual court will never grant mercy to me nor you alone

Oh, when I saw you there, you silly giggly thing ,
in a Portobello courtyard stuffed with dolls,
I knew I wouldn't escape the glitter of my destiny,
The shiny trinkets in the jaws of your scrutiny,
The totem pole of this finality, and it was
then they had dinner for us on the upper floor of
your dwelling and the rest is history...


Do you know that *nani* means " thank you" in Malayan
and that the Tamiils are not really black?
Was that fieldwork in Madagascar really a lesson in anxiety?
And is this European field-work tougher than the other aboriginal,
Ethical ground where they feed us to the sharks and larks
disappearing in light dusk of the British lakes?
How could they ever think we were just
Some fakes

*Roller-Skating Notes*

Feeding ourselves on tons of pure
Chocolate, out of sadness?
We are 99 percent, you said,
And I say that Exile is 100 percent torture, mixed with the powder of Oblivion

reading sadness;
Language is space pointing at geometry of our souls
down by Ashbery's lacustrine
Cities and
Up beyond Joycean silent hills,
where verse is in labor,
Delivering a child of street speech,
Without punctuation. And you,
with those bright feathers that
You placed up the totem pole near the canoe, floating down that

Aboriginal river of your singing voice...
Wait, are we the strangers all this young in here? Coming
From some very, very young
And infantile tribe?
And what are we to do with the shamans dealing with
Stupidity and administration, in every damned shtetl we passed through?

As if the algebra of heartache had

## Nina Zivancevic

To knock down every wall
And every barbed wire we ran into…
The comfort of strangers is
The pivotal moment of deep sleep,
Into which I sink having met the Big Other
who tends to your architectural structural network
Where the intuition slumbers
And the doors of perceptive dungeon
Open up;
It was Vienna,
And it was 1893…
My ankle was broken and your mind elsewhere;
Hey, the King of silly laughter,
Listen to your heartbeat:
Tick   tack   tick   tack   tick tack   and yes, tick
The answer after which
This world is not going to be better off
It's not going to save the poor
But just decorate them
With the Maori shells
Instead of money
And was it Shakespeare who had seen us all in a huge dungeon?
And was it Andrew Marvell who laughed it off with his
Ha ha ha ha ha ha

*Roller-Skating Notes*

On his lost road to Damascus?
And was it John Donne who could have done without the world

Painted all in green hues and shadows?
Pkk and Kobané are surely not going to
Survive without you, so you need not hold onto your colonial stick and

That trickster's top hat, and
In this Temple here,
In this god—forlorn shtetl,
I'm in a courtroom full of flowers.
The spiritual court is in session
And some red liquid leaking from the ante-chamber of
my heart. Shhhhhh…
The violins are playing and Chagall
Is playing chess with Duchamp….

Exile is such a long nonsensical thing, your majesty,
And this Song of Songs
Is about to shut my screen off, and just before it all ends now,
Now you should know—that
In order to give, one has to really get,
That instant of music

## Nina Zivancevic

Oozing from the crack
In the Tree of life painted in Kabbalah
Ah, the tree, my King of Davids,
And the soft breeze from the Mediterranean cliffs,
so
Elohim and Elohena, thus
To life!
Elohim and Elohena
 and thus,
to life!!
Elohim,
Elohim, Elohena,
I see Him,
The way I see
You,
the huge
Speckle of light
In the radiant Temple
washed in light!

*Dawnbreak in Paris, October 14, 2015*

*Roller-Skating Notes*

## CONFESSIONS OF A FALLEN ANGEL, NIETZSCHEAN SONG

It was so easy to penetrate the monastery
Everyone there admired the span of my burned
 charcoaled wings
I was the best at pushing the metaphor
To the utmost insanity
The semi-daemons were lighting candles for my
 well-being
While eyeing me with a mocking eye: now, come to
 think...

what idiot would still
Carry the torch and light up the road
When all other angels
Smoke hookahs and sell dope
—they were allowed every folly—
They said they were innocent
And sexless, good-intended while unaware
Of their deeds..
I knew it: They would not put my name
Into any Evangelist book unless
They wanted to criticize it

# Nina Zivancevic

While awaiting on the Almighty

To flush favors upon them

And the local mortals

Paint their image on their icons..

They said "we had given him Light, trusted him

With that precious stuff

And he had just burnt stars with it,

That evil angel,

 that bad bad

unworthy man."

*Roller-Skating Notes*

## CHOPIN
(body without organs)

Body without organs is hard to describe or conquer
It brings me back not so much to Deleuze and Zizek but back to Chopin
whose body was buried at Père Lachaise but his heart- (his sister did it)
into the Baroque cathedral of St Cross in Warsaw.
And many organs were buried like that
Ashes in cathedrals, empty grave of Vasko da Gama in Cochin
tombs of many other saints whose deeds exist only in legends
They evaporated into thin air
Why do people want to ground a corpse?
What are they going to do with the spirit?
How do you ground the spirit?

Into a national history book?
Or, in the case of composers, could it be a history of music books?

There's no need to leave any corporal trace,
whatever we do in life, we are doing it
while we are doing it.

*Roller-Skating Notes*

## HANNAH ARENDT

"What I meant by banality is  superficiality of Eichmann-
that's what I call evil

His banality—his refusal to imagine the life of others
How other people live—that's evil"

She didn't know she was Jewish, her family didn't tell her
as they were not religious

They were "the apatrides"

Once pushed out of their countries- the refugees, the
stateless become

"the scum of the earth "(Arendt )

Stateless person  a refugee   has no rights; he is worse
Than a person in his own country and in jail who has
some rights

Lying being committed as necessity

Is a crime,  a psychological crime

Which cannot be justified—

She was interned in a French camp in 1940 but unlike
Weil, she survived.

## Nina Zivancevic

EVIL is not only
Conscientious, it is also sentimental penetration of that
    strategy of living on one's own
i mean that ability to speak on one's own
Like she did  and
against the Jews who collaborated
with the Nazis

## SMARTPHONE

No fixed term bullshit job per se
Any job can turn into a bullshit job
Or a dream job
It depends on the treatment of the worker in question!!
But how do you treat me?
Your smartphone smarter than you have ever been—it turned itself on
Was turned on by itself
And called me this morning
2016

Nina Zivancevic

IF I WERE TO PAINT

My interior
would be ocher
yellow and red
a deep deep dark
Fissure
Between these two
a dark memory
A dark legacy
From the Persians

*Roller-Skating Notes*

## RELIGIOUS DREAM

Empty scyscrapers over the suburb of Belgrade where I used to live as a kid . Three quarters of the landscape's background are filled with early morning clouds and it is there where your dainty face emerges, somewhat solemn , sprinkled with tired wrinkles and recent internet memories.
You keep staring at my tiny early morning breasts sweating , showing up slowly behind the covers, my light blue hair falls slightly over my Rembrandt cheek…I know this Andre Breton look on your face, after all you are un Breton, in search of his Celtic counterpart and we are in the land of the Celts. You search for my hand but it is hidden between my legs where total intimacy, total madness, writing for its own sake  are hidden and where your dreams of abandoned childhood sleep covered under my sweaty blankets.

Ohhh, you are kissing me at the spot where I think that it will hurt, total intimacy always hurts,your lips on the opening of my vagina, where have you been? Why did I wait for you for so long and now that you have appeared here, why do I feel so sleepy?
You are fast like a Mexican jaguar, you move in me with grace, and you try to reach that spot which was never en-

tered before. By no one. It's like a secret photograph which speaks to you at the moment when you start hearing the cries of the seagulls, the heat of the dessert thickens and I see your sweat on your weary brow embedded with theories. These are your instant cookies which you pop into your mouth around noon, as I shiver, sitting quietly on the top of your dick then moving slowly. You are my perpetuum mobile and I adore you, ach und ach, shrieking loudly and ever louder until you lift up your hand and cover my mouth with the back of your palm…"are you happy now?"You ask me, then having noticed that I nodded my head, satisfied, you take my other hand, that one which is not covered with sweat, and you take me out. For a walk. We should feed the cat first, you say. And then the dog, and then the parakeets. They are totally innocent ..so different from us, you say. You are my church, you say. And you, my religion, I add. I have never seen so much zeal, so much enthusiasm like I've seen in you this morning. You are my palace of the utmost discovery , you finally say, carefully locking the door behind us and I feel like a schoolgirl, that I am, trotting behind you along a cobbled street.

## POLITICALLY CORRECT

He spoke of everything but
Of the immigration,
Not of migrants,
Not of exiles
Not of the terror imposed
On the terrorists
He asked "who are these people
stealing books from the libraries?"
He didn't use his trumpet to blear at Trump..
He was the most important "language poet"
Of them all…
2017

Nina Zivancevic

## FRANC LISZT'S HOUSE
*(December 2015)*

Liszt was convinced that absolute music and vocal music
are so picturesque on their own and can express anything
that a realistic staging of a musical composition is
unnecessary or even decreases the value and its effect.

He felt that soul is able to imagine much more than we
 could ever show it.
Liszt considered the oratorio to be of a higher aesthetic
quality than the opera.

Hans von Bulow gave perfect description of the place of
Ferentz Liszt. Holds in music history: he said he
 reformed
the spiritual drama, created a new type of oratorio
resulting in a genre very much like Wagner's opera. Liszt
was against putting his oratorio on stage...

As much as Bruckner started his inner life in a
monastery, Liszt ended his own in a convent- the most
 prominent
piece in his house was the prayer stand.

*Roller-Skating Notes*

## MAYBE THE SPRING

Was still possible
In its dialectic impossibility
Tristan is gone, in comes his Alter Ego, Batman,
to entertain with his winter song
speaking of power and his entertaining disinterest ,
Wagner should have known better about
The silence and soft reflection…

Alas, they will all leave this note of Sol major
Where another German sang so many happy songs,
Even his Requiem was cheerful, as it spoke of
Persistence of Death and memory.

Now, maybe the spring will bring us back the swallows,
The petals of cherry-trees, the smell of poisonous ivy,
My memory of expressionism where
The migrants were hungry and asking for bread..
But where is the trace of intimacy, smeared over my heart
Like a stale lipstick; no,
No , not wine in it, the wine is for the swine
And even von Karajan should lower his hands

## Nina Zivancevic

To conduct a softer intermezzo...
Yes, maybe the spring
Will come to the street again, that is,
If I get a ladder from the housing authorities I will descend
from my balcony
Into the garden
In the midst of this polluted fog...

*Roller-Skating Notes*

## THERE'S SOMETHING

There's something you
can never forgive me
and something
I can never
Forgive you
And that's mainly our
Rigidity of not
Being able to forgive

Nina Zivancevic

## BERGSON, ON THE EDGE OF POSITIVE THINKING

So if we close our eyes shall
We see the same shade of the blue
Which we see on your painting?
Shall i be sad that my son has gone
Into his reckless adventure
Or shall i be happy to get a brand new daughter?
Should i feel sorry that i felt obliged
To leave that soulful event or simply
Delighted that i had a chance to
Be there when it started happening?
Shall i feel heavy that my pockets got
Emptied or simply relieved that i
Did not have to worry about my possessions any longer?
And if i have not recently dwelled with angels, i was
   hanging out with
Their less fortunate brothers, so
Reckless  wordly and  sublime..

## IF

So I know if
I push away this midnight
Inside of me
Peek through the screen of fog
And inhuman guts
I'll be able to continue
Writing
Poetry

Nina Zivancevic

## SOON I'LL BE BACK

"Soon I'll be back," he said…
And then when another one tried
that trick on me- I knew it
wouldn't work,
in fact, what a jerk, to think that
the trick would work on me!
In fact, the PP syndrome is
a difficult thing to get rid of-
PP meaning the Persian prince, or
he was called "just smile and wink"
when all other folks tried to survive: hunger, flood
voyage by the sea, sharks,
editorial darts, cooing of the doves
or were they pigeons? Or were they
mag pies? Or were they ravens?

BIRDS OF FEATHER FLOCK TOGETHER
was their slogan, and
i was an eagle on my own…

*Roller-Skating Notes*

## AN OPEN LETTER TO A VERY VERY STRAWBERRY FRIEND

In one of your letters you blasted
"You were one of us I thought , Nin, and then you disappeared ".
I could not live in a family without manners though
How could I? And I don't mean petty burg manners,
form eating its substance and so on
It's more like I needed caring
In Europe though,
I felt some sort of caring that I did not get in the U.S.
However ever and How :
Over there I had more lovers to tell my nightmarish night stories to--
Or were these stories my true lovers?
Once
upon
a time

Nina Zivancevic

## CONTACT IMPROVISATION

Movement and sound exercise
Is utopia sort of …ever idealistic
The Living Theater used it, then abused it
That was Joe Chaikin's exercise but
The concept of bare stage is purely Brecht's
Just voice and body
They are never at war though, and never against the sets
Just as: there is NO money for the elaborate sets
They became prominent, like in
Grotowski's poor theater, but hey,
What does resistance mean today?
You have to have the top and also the bottom,
and
that is …a class structure

*Roller-Skating Notes*

## FOR MY DEAD LOST AND FORLORN FRIEND

You inhabit
That special hidden nook in my heart
From that unseen and never heard of space-- you never depart
I placed you on the top of Pantheon
Where you've always dwelled from the beginingless time
Ahoy! Justly or unjustly so
You've been my eyes to see the world
My ears who had heard the nicest music of them all
You've been my mouth and my voice who spoke poetry all the time...
And to say that I ve always loved you so
Is just another way to say: without you, I'm completely lost...
And the life goes on, and these words.
.I've been kinda repeating them every couple of years or so

Nina Zivancevic

And Ira and Beba and Maya and Elio and Gera and
Philippe and Radovan and Zoran and Luka
And now you- please. sail gently into that light,
you'll join the best
and the rest will
madly love you

*Roller-Skating Notes*

## ERRARE HUMANUM EST, PERSEVERARE DIABOLICUM
( latin proverb)

One of these days
You'll start watching football games
And it will be over
Although i could go
To my skating ring in return
I could attend the skating rink
Of my mind
I could make all these Imaginary
Wish-me-well figures and you'll
Be there, behind your camera, where else, framing my figures while
Trying to remember how to sing
"I love you song"...just for me:
See, we're in Russia and it's 1904
And my grandma has just dropped
A handkerchief , on purpose
Hoping your grandpa would pick it up..

## Nina Zivancevic

Yes, like Ira Cohen said once
You may not believe in Karma street
But i've surely walked down that one
And that's the only thing you'll
Get from me,
With Much Love,
nina Zee

### Roller-Skating Notes

## IT'S A HOLLYWOOD DRAMA
*(for Alice Notley)*

and these are Hollywood babes, my Poetry teacher said
Chris Kraus and Eileen Myles and Kathy Acker who re-
placed the mythic girls Hedda Lamar, lana Turner and
    Marlene Dietrich, as

Their TV Producers also believed in the Dream of a
    literary persona.

But did they have as much fun while writing their stuff, as
    much fun as we did,

in NYC that summer?i asked.
Oh yes, my Teacher said, but they believed in a different
    sort of fun, they 're different from us.
i know this much by now, I know that something keeps
    us here, in a French restaurant,

staring at the clouds
Howling at the moon

## Nina Zivancevic

Serving our kids
Serving Community at large , soon they will call us
Maudit poets, strange birds, forever and ever,
forever we refused
to sell quickly
our songs

## MY CHILDHOOD

The first time i got that protect-art spray
I sprayed all my father's paintings
He, like the rest of my beloved artists
Whose work hangs on my wall- had never thought of posterity
They left all their work open
Unprotected and raw like they were themselves
And i always wanted to protect them
Thus i found myself on a Freud's couch
I... I ...i..
My dad.. Dad ....dead father
And my dead lovers...
I see your motherly nature
(The shrink said),
You must had suffered a great personal loss
In your childhood

Nina Zivancevic

## PAPA ERIC LE TENDRE
## AND JOAQUÍN GUZMAN ( EL CHAPO)
## ARE MY HEROS

Papa Eric-
you don't have to sell advice and
Red balloons on a subway
We love you
As we long to hear your song
From the edge of the bush
You sleep on the subway bench
Covered with mice shit and roaches
You say "tell no one that I love you
They will be even more jealous"
Papa Eric no one can love me the
Way you do I am out of nowhere
And no place to go
Just like you

*Roller-Skating Notes*

## EL CHAPO

So they think they got you
And el Zorro and Che and Fidel Castro
And if they keep you inside the wall
Street dungeon/who is going to supply drugs to the Wall
  Street lawyers
They cannot function without your coke and yerba buena
and for
The mescal alone the intellectuals from all these white
countries
will surely set you free
Perhaps you overdid it in your daily supply of the
  autonomous power
You audited that mister invisible
And gave him the wrong stuff
Your pay was getting smaller and smaller and your family's
  debt taller
You... Hey I do not know
Where you, senor  el Chapo,  went wrong
But I know the prisons in California
Can be comfortable, if enough of your pals sit in them too

## Nina Zivancevic

Watch out for razor blades hidden in a loaf of bread
And don't take too many common showers
You are el prenz y el GATO,
Lord of any drug war in town;
You are no terrorist babe and the prayer rug is safe under your feet
It's all the matter of money and some wrong payola
And those who should be in jail instead … and who rule the world,
Will need you soon to be out, doing some dirty job for them.

You dealt directly with the coke kings of Colombia
who flew the stuff from the Andean jungles to Mexico,
each of their planes carrying à ton of product and then in
NO time you used to
 smuggle that greed into California…
They called you El Rapido,
Just now…
Listen to the song Guantanamera and
Soon, you will be at large and
    riding the pampas again.

*Roller-Skating Notes*

## THE BALLAD OF STENKA RAZIN

Did i call you my soul or my spirit or my mind
L'esprit, l'ame et le coeur
All fits into the common expression i use when i call you *Dusha maya*...

See this is something the Westerners can't dig into
The dog in me spelled out yet another story
In which i rush through the door like a dodo, like an early morning casualty

Yes that's me, female Stenka Razin whose real image is wrought by Ivan Rebroff's heavinly voice
What happened to Razin, to me and Billy the kid is something that only Robin hood knows
And none of the anarchists you frequent here and now,
It happened that i wasnt born into
Your great "kovski" club which allows
You to shoot chairs, stars and floating clouds, the act which in turn, makes me Love

You guys, Tarkovski, Bela Tar and you, camarade

# Nina Zivancevic

Merejkowski

And it's only normal i hang with your gang of the riders
In the storm

Into this world were thrown
Like a dog without a bone,
Riders in the storm.

## THEM RUSSIANS

Russian Jews do not accept migrants,
They are crazy the way my dad was.
Port parole says we will not be like Egypt who don't respect the convention,
she says, we will accept them...
A lady in there says: this becomes Afrika! It's not Israel any more!!
The other polit-activist says: after Shoah , you should be ashamed to even
Mention such a thing
Hotline is against Human Trafficking of organs
The Israeli Tribunal, like any other- full of
Honest and dishonest lawyers
A police woman says to a man: although it is not written on your visa, you can work,
They just close their eyes to the fact that the Eritrean and Sudanese migrants
are not allowed to work.
"When it comes to expulsion," the activist says," it is disgusting that
These Eritreans and the Sudanese are expelled from

the Ministry of interior and not.. the Nigerians or the
Ghanaians who can return peaceful to their "bled"
Story of a Baule man who wants to transfer and bury his
Beté wife
He had to show to the other tribe that he didn't kill her
there in Israel

*Roller-Skating Notes*

## TRIPLE SORROW

I knew i was no good
To go to that Vienna conference
Where the lifeless camp of
Unfriendly creatures discussed
My dearest and the nearest by using the method of
   a zany academic vivisection

Alas! And those who underwent their judgment
they were all dead and i had to
bear the results of their work's final
artificial autopsy, and in that trickle now, barely alive…
But whatever happened there, did not make me stronger
In fact : their ignorant reasoning killed me
Or killed my desire to see the Imperial City of Vienna
   in a new or

Different light, see, I almost got married there once
But the rabbi refused to listen to my bridegroom's story;
His grandparents born in this city, suffocated or
   slaughtered
My grandmother as well– in an era which all folks tried

to forget.

I did not have a violin to play over the Viennese rooves
   that year
But i've heard its sound in an empty loft today
And i saw Chagall's face when i closed my eyes
And i've heard both Allen and Ira
Whispering" get out of here kiddo",
jealousy is for the sub-species, and IT feeds
On green feathers , on pork cutlets and
on bad scholarship.

*Roller-Skating Notes*

NOW YOU SEE IT—NOW YOU DON'T SEE IT
*(true account of Gregory Corso)*

Once I met Gregory in Boulder, Colorado,
showed him my translations of his poetry which he found
beautiful and wanted to try my Taurus ring on,
Now you see it- now you don't see it, he said.
It took Ginsberg two months to return my ring to me.
Once I met Gregory in NYC after my incredible marijuana arrest,
And having heard my story, he took 400 dollars
from his left boot where he kept money and gave it to me
"take it, kid, you'd need it for the lawyers"; the story of the ring forgotten;
The last time I saw him in New York,
I was with my dad, buying a TV set,
When Gregory jumped on us, out of nowhere,
cursing the commercial habits of high capitalism- " don't

## Nina Zivancevic

you come from

Europe folks," he yelled, "don't you have some taste and elegance?

You don't need this junk to fill your brain with non-seeeense", he said

And then disappeared into Astor place
muggy dust for ever..

*Roller-Skating Notes*

## POEM FOR EM

Self-control is what you need,
and Character," my Love said while
slamming the door
behind a small clinic on boulevard
Malesherbes in Paris
…now it's raining and it's cold and
I am in pain.
—"You have three days to check in here
and solve this problem" the doctor said "otherwise
every–thing is going to burst."
 …and it did.. the cysts, the time, the money, the lovers.
My lover called me last night to tell me
How much he missed me—
He sent me a poem he wrote for me
In a computer program which I could not open

## Nina Zivancevic

Just at the time I believed I could have
A heart-opener for everyone's heart;
My Love had heard my Lover calling and asked:
"Who's THAT calling you, in the middle of the night?"
"It's a young poet bursting with impatience," I said,
"he did not mean to do you any harm…"
—The doctor's looked at me and gasped:
"All this growth is at the point of necrosis- it's going to burst

soon and then…it won't be so pretty…"
This love story is going to last – forever although it could
Burst out any second and burn my soul
And then – it won't be so pretty…
—They injected the scanner liquid into
my veins – my blood got warmer,
I lifted up my hands….
His face lit by moonlight, his thick black
Hair on my stomach,
The blood got warmer and warmer
WE kissed and kissed through the moonlight, his
Sweet saliva, his ultra-light kisses, his hard hard cock
Inside of me
"Come my love, he said, - let us
    come together …"

### Roller-Skating Notes

"The scanner is over", the doctor said, "and
you were lucky- you were not allergic
to this product.."
HIS face in semi-light over my
Sweaty thighs, his fingers on my nipples,
My face on his soft abdomen, this love which
Last forever...
Oh! My wet superb love!
We could not stop
Touching each other
Ever since we met!
"THE growth is less significant on
The left side of the ovaries than on the right one",
the doc said,
"Don't worry, doc – if you have to cut me up, just
go ahead, I AM such an obedient patient,
but the idea that my body
turns into a salad – just doesn't make me smile..."
"I don't want to be tender, I don't want you
to caress me – I want you to destroy me", Trakl's sister
told the poet, and I wanted you
to crush me and then lick me away
and cover with kisses...
"It's very addictive after a while," my good friend

## Nina Zivancevic

told me "once you start
with heavy erotica you can never stop –
until death
      do us
            part –
And now the doc awaits for me there
On the other side
          Of heaven

*Roller-Skating Notes*

## ABJECT/DÉBRIS ART 1.

One day I stopped loving it. I felt being its only representation, representative and a uniformed statue . I was the only replica of my own insane creation, I became a dated caricature of my old powerful but degenerated self, a piece of Debris art admired by the connoisseurs of the Abject a long ago. I knew the death was around the corner, now that I had almost 75 to 80 percent of my friends 'names and references crossed out in my telephone book. I did not complain though and accepted begrudgingly this fact, shrugged my shoulders with a long "sooo what.." I find myself presently on a bus rushing from Beograd to Paris (the Easter vacation's over and lots of children, kids of the forlorn Serbs and Gypsies living in Diaspora are eager to get back home although, very few of them knew exactly where their home was). To be honest, the same goes for me: I ve had a vague idea where I was heading to-- I was heading to the place where I would see, once upon a time–lots of art–and, as I was heading, to a place where I was watching a lot of good movies with my kid. Or was that the place an epithomy of laughter, soft evenings, sweet gatherings with the like minded friends,where we, armed with gin and absinthe, shared our latest verses, news, gossip No point of return there. With a certain geometrical progression in their mad speed of disappearance–my buddies left the battlefield and in Paris I dwelled all alone. The morning television program from television channel ARTE would vaguely disperse the deadly silence which reigned my apartment. ... And the monotonous sound of the cell phone would, sort of start bleeping on its own, urging me to dial one or two numbers which were still left intact in my book, I mean they remained uncrossed on page, shining through. But who were those people anyways?

xxxx

Certainly, they were not my buddies, the folks whose brilliance marked my existence and whose presence in art and science—as much as in my life—meant so much to me, alas! Such rare treasures in my life tended to disappear in huge lumps, they all oozed down the drain.. And first of all they were replaced by those fore mentioned dummies... who did not qualify as real partners in my scholarly meditations and then. Slowly but surely those disappeared from my horizon as well—one thing for sure, among all imitative qualities in life, real affection and camaradery cannot be invoked and faked easily on a daily basis. You call people and you see one another, but you both know that it's a fake. Like a fake fur or a plastic cake, you have a taste of the real thing, you still remember its original shape and size but sadly enough you attest to the fact that this encounter between you two IS NOT IT, not the real thing you treasured so much and remembered. So that's how I found myself in the utmost lonileness in the most solitary town on Earth and that was Paris. Oh, the loneliness of the long distance runner, the film by Tony Richardson, how I knew you well!

## Roller-Skating Notes

Perhaps never did it strike me with such clarity, with such desperate unforgiving clarity as it did this morning, while riding on this quiet bus with the spring breakers munching their forlorn sandwitches–I was under the special sepulchral impression that my life was this time–definitively over. I finished it, ruined by my utmost speed–like I was running somewhere–could not determine exactly where. but I was rushing to get over there and I was burnt out in my own endeavour , Burnt by my own speed which propelled me to get there, anywhere–AHEAD of my own time! This discovery almost made me laugh- and I rushed to call that special friend, confidant to my lonely efforts–but hmmm–there was no one to reach out for. I was heading to my own dystopian nest in the heart of Montnartre, but I dreaded opening its doors of perception, at that particular place where my physical home was,where I dwelled in Paris, in the 17th arrondissement where also my very heart of hearts and my memories were locked , But I lost the key to that door and was never happy while sleeping, eating or working.

Nina Zivancevic

## ABJECT/DEBRIS 2.

Although Andzey Wajda says in his last great film "BlueFlowers" that the frontier between politics and art should not be erased, we feel that the world we live in forbids its citizens to ignore the effects of global political and eco-logical issues. The face of Art(s) becomes dirty and ugly to those who tend to its overwhelming neoliberal, commercial Endeavours and who ignore the burning issues of humanity. Oliver Ressler's work, especially the documentaries of this contemporary Austrian filmmaker cum activist and performance artist reveal his humanist obsession with Human misery and hardship. Artur Zmijewski is another responsible filmmaker–he filmed the now–burned "Jungle" refugee camp in Calais...otherwise known as the shame on the face of France, and shame on the face of greedy England. The question which another one, Le Grice, asks in his book Shoot Shoot Shoot: the First Decade of the London Film-makers' Co-operative 1966-76, for example is "whether any aspect of illusion or sequential narrational structure can be made compatible with the anti-illusionist materialistic aesthetics?" In other words, how can we watch the Cloud(s), talk about the clouds, film them and at the same time not pay for them, not worry about them being polluted, not disappear inside of them for a lot of money etc etc.. Yes, how can we live... in it (the existential dread?)

*Roller-Skating Notes*

## PRAGUE 89 ...BUDAPEST   BUKAREST
## WARSOVIE   BELGRADE

*(17 November in Prague)*

The soviet invasion was terrible everywhere
In its more explicit forms in Prague
Bratislava Bukarest Warsaw and Budapest
And in its more subtle forms in
Belgrade Zagreb Ljubljana
Lenin had said on his dearhbed: YOU should never allow
Staljin to get My job
But Staljin did
And then Krushchov
Who saved Solženjicin's life nontheless
I remember My father The director of The national
museum in Belgrade said : what you will see now
YOU should never forget
He was pushing The banknotes into the toothpaste
while we were crossing the Yugoslav and Italian borders
at Udine
YOU should not forget The turqoise sky over Venice,
The greeness of Tintoreto's paintings the blue hues of
  Veronese

The pale nuance of Boticelli

## Nina Zivancevic

Once we reenter the CITY of Belgrade
We may never see them again
The blueness of the sky
Red red gondolas
Staljin rules all our countries east of here and Tito had
signed with him a very messy deal..
We returned to Belgrade safely but
Dad had lost his job soon after that
I left the country soon after Tito's death
I know that Milosevic was poisoned in his cell in
  The Hague

And that Zoran Djindjic was shot in his courtyard
Now we have Trump's walls and Putin's drones
However
I know that all the serbian checzk hungarian slovaque
rumanian slovenian macedonian polish national and the
international underground avangardes are
My sisters and brothers
I know it when i see it
So
Long live anarchy
And the spirit of our
Daily resistance

*Roller-Skating Notes*

## PARIS IS BURNING

Paris is burning
The buildings are in flames
 kids, cars, faces- shame on color
Shame on white   shame   on  black shame
Everyone is burning with shame

Let me tell you mother, why
Paris is burning, says he,
Let me tell you mother why Paris
Is burning- the police have set children
On fire, the police have set children on fire as
These  were tired of social injustice
As they were sick with social injustice

Let me tell you mother why Paris is burning- the police
Have set black kids on fire and they turned red, they
turned gray
They turned to burnt flesh
Just because they are black
Let me tell you why Paris is burning,
Nothing bad will happen to me, mother

As I am white, and yet
I understand why Paris is burning,
Kids, buildings, cars and faces
Burning with shame…

(written circa 2005)

*Roller-Skating Notes*

Nina Zivancevic

Nina Zivancevic

## ABOUT THE AUTHOR

Poet, essayist, fiction writer, playwright, art critic, translator and contributing editor to NY ARTS magazine from Paris, Serbian-born Nina Zivancevic published 15 books of poetry. She has also written three books of short stories, two novels and a book of essay on Milosh Crnjanski (her doctoral thesis) published in Paris, New York and Belgrade. The recipient of three literary awards, a former assistant and secretary to Allen Ginsberg, she has also edited and participated in numerous anthologies of contemporary world poetry.

As editor and correspondent she has contributed to *New York Arts Magazine, Modern Painters, American Book Review, East Village Eye, Republique de lettres*. She has

*Roller-Skating Notes*

lectured at Naropa University, New York University, the Harriman Institute and St.John's University in the U.S., and she has taught English language and literature at La Sorbonne (Paris I and V) and the History of Avant-garde Theatre at Paris 8 University in France and at numerous universities and colleges in Europe.

She has actively worked for theatre and radio: 4 of her plays were performed and emitted in the U.S. and Great Britain.

In New York she had worked with the "Living Theatre" and the members of the "Wooster Group".

She lives and works in Paris.

www.ingramcontent.com/pod-product-compliance
Lightning Source LLC
Chambersburg PA
CBHW021444080526
44588CB00009B/675